The Rockwool Foundation Research Unit

The impact of incentives and interview methods on response quantity and quality in diary- and booklet-based surveys

Jens Bonke
Peter Fallesen

University Press of Southern Denmark
Odense 2009

The impact of incentives and interview methods on response quantity and quality in diary- and booklet-based surveys

Study Paper No. 25

Published by:
© The Rockwool Foundation Research Unit and
University Press of Southern Denmark

Copying from this book is permitted only within
institutions that have agreements with CopyDan,
and only in accordance with the limitations laid
down in the agreement

Address:
The Rockwool Foundation Research Unit
Sejroegade 11
DK-2100 Copenhagen Oe

Telephone	+45 39 17 38 32
Fax	+45 39 20 52 19
E-mail	forskningsenheden@rff.dk
Home page	www.rff.dk
ISBN	978-87-90199-21-0
ISSN	0908-3979
September 2009	
Print run:	300
Printed by	Special-Trykkeriet Viborg a-s
Price:	60.00 DKK, including 25% VAT

Contents

Abstract 5
1. Introduction 7
2. Background 9
3. Data and method 13
4. Results 17
   A. Descriptive statistics 17
   B. Response quantity – incentives and methods............ 20
   C. Response quality – incentives and methods............. 23
5. Conclusion 29
Bibliography... 31

The impact of incentives and interview methods on response quantity and quality in diary- and booklet-based surveys

Jens Bonke – Peter Fallesen

Abstract

This paper investigates the impact on response quantity and quality of a diary- and booklet-based survey of using different interview methods and lottery prizes. In addition to a conventional questionnaire on background and time-use-related characteristics, the survey included time-diaries for adult household members and children over six years of age, and a booklet for recording the previous month's spending by the household. The respondents could choose to use either CATI (Computer-Assisted Telephone Interviewing) or web-based CAPI (Computer-Assisted Personal Interviewing) for the different parts of the survey. Lottery prizes for participants were drawn every month. The amount of these prizes was varied during the survey period, and for some respondents the prizes were doubled if they had used only the CAPI method. The response rate was significantly affected by the size of the lottery prizes, and the doubling of these prizes for using the web had a tremendous impact on the number of respondents choosing this method. The response quality did not vary systematically with the size of the lottery prizes *per se*, but the quality did increase as a result of the impact on the number of web interviews, because this method was found to yield a significantly higher quality for the diary, booklet and questionnaire information.

Jens Bonke, seniorresearcher, and Peter Fallesen, research assistant, are members of the staff of the Rockwool Foundation Research Unit, Sejroegade 11, DK-2100 Copenhagen, Denmark. The authors thank Rob Alessie and the other participants of the MESS workshop in Zeist, August 2008, the participants at a research seminar at the Rockwool Foundation Research Unit (in particular Lars Højsgaard Andersen), participants at the methodology seminar at the Department of Sociology, University of Copenhagen, June 2009, and in particular Professor Eskil Wadensjö for refereeing the paper. Any mistakes or errors remain the responsibility of the authors. This study was funded by the Rockwool Foundation.
E-mail address for correspondence with Jens Bonke: jb@rff.dk

1. Introduction

In parallel with the recent trend towards conducting ever more surveys, there has also been a decline in the response rates, making it harder to obtain the desired number of completed interviews for these surveys (Hansen, 2006; Curtin et al., 2005; de Leeuw & de Heer, 2002). At the same time, the world wide web has become more frequently used for survey data collection, because most people in developed countries now have access to the internet and the use of the web is less costly than surveying by ordinary mail or telephone. The drawback of web surveying, however, is that the response rates are usually even lower than those obtained by the conventional data collection methods (Couper, 2000; Dillman & Bowker, 2001), though some findings do indicate the opposite in certain studies (Schneider et al., 2002; Crawford et al. 2002). As the quality of survey estimates is contingent on a high response rate, this problem has prompted the introduction of various incentives aimed at obtaining a greater number of completed interviews.

Incentives used in surveys with the aim of increasing the response rates are manifold, varying from sending letters in advance and increasing the number of reminder calls to pre-interview payments, cash incentives, charitable donations, and the chance to win lottery prizes. In many surveys the financial incentives are small in monetary terms and with respect to the chances of winning those distributed by lottery, and the impact on response rates has been found to be relatively limited, making these initiatives less cost-effective than originally anticipated (Göritz, 2004).

Moreover, evaluations of the impact of the incentives used in surveys and of the impact of applying different survey methods – mail, telephone, web – usually focus on response rates – the quantitative outcomes – leaving undetermined the effect on the quality of the replies to the questions in the surveys – the qualitative outcomes.

On the basis of a large-scale Danish timeuse and consumption survey, which included a questionnaire, diaries and a booklet, we have tested within an experimental design the impact of different financial incentives and interview methods on the quantity (response rates) and quality (accuracy) of the results achieved. Lottery prizes introduced at the beginning of the survey were increased considerably during the final six months in order to encourage people to participate. To measure the impact of lottery prizes as an incentive for participants to switch from telephone interviews to the web, the prizes were doubled for participants who used the latter method instead of the former for all the instruments of the survey, i.e. the questionnaire, the diaries, and the booklet.

The time-diary instrument was designed not only for adults but also for children above the age of six years. To increase the response rates among children and young people, the randomly selected IPs in the second half of the survey period were told in the advance letter that the chances of winning a lottery prize increased with the number of participating respondents, inclusive of spouses and children within the household.

In the next section, the background for this paper is further discussed, with references to other evaluations. Then follows a section on the data and methods used in this evaluation. The results section includes descriptive statistics about response rates for the different instruments used, as well as statistical analyses of the impact of the financial incentives on response quantity and quality. The final section offers some conclusions.

2. Background

The general decline in household survey response rates in recent decades, see for example Curtin et al. (2005) and de Leeuw & de Heer (2002), has led to growing concern about the ability of household survey data to represent the behaviour of the population, due to possible selection biases. There are different reasons for the increasing non-response rates. In part they are due to the increasing number of private and public surveys demanding more of people's time, and thus overburdening them; and in part they are due to an increase in working hours among employed people, making them more time-constrained. Both factors result in people becoming more selective in what they choose to participate in, with the result that for some surveys they end up as refusals or non-contact persons (Groves & Couper, 1998). For surveys including time-use information, as in this case, this lack of available time might be a major problem simply because busy people are less frequently at home, thus decreasing the contact rates – and, at the same time, these busy people may be less willing to take the time to participate in a survey, thus increasing the refusal rate. In addition, people with weak community ties may also respond less often than other people to surveys (Robinson & Godbey, 1997; Abraham et al., 2006). In the first case, the lack of participation by busy people, the bias may lead to an underestimation of hours worked in the population, and in the latter case, the lack of participation by people with weak community ties, the result might be an overestimation of hours spent on volunteer work (Abraham et al., 2006).

Although the busy people hypothesis has been rejected by Pääkkönen (1999) and actually reversed by Robinson (1999), who found that busy people are more likely to participate than less busy people in time-use surveys, and thus that non-response is therefore not necessarily a source of bias in survey estimates (Groves, 2006), different strategies have been introduced to increase participation rates, including the introduction of both financial and non-financial incentives and the use of more efficient interview instruments such as the world wide web.

Various incentives that refine the data collection tools have been introduced to counter the problem of falling response rates in surveys. Advance letters explaining the importance for society of doing research on a specified topic, with the research being made possible through survey information, is one method used to convince people to participate, together with information about how much (or little) time the survey is likely to take. In addition, increasing the number of follow-up calls is used as a method of increasing response rates. The impact of advance letters on response rates, however, is mixed, with Hembroff et al. (2005) finding a positive and significant impact but Singer et al. (2000) coming up with no significant impact. The announcement of a long interview, however, has been found to decrease the response rate significantly, independently of the kind of incentive given (Hansen, 2006).

Among prepaid rewards for participating in surveys, scratch cards are one of the most popular, because the recipient cannot resist scratching the card and thereafter feels obligated to participate in the survey irrespective of whether or not he/she has won a prize. Personal in-kind gifts are also used as prepaid rewards, particularly in commercial surveys. Rewards given after participation include cash paid directly to the respondent and charitable donations made on behalf of the respondent to, for example, the Red Cross or Médecins sans Frontières if the questionnaire is submitted. Warriner et al. (1996) and Armstrong (1975) showed that only prepaid cash incentives have a positive impact on response rates, while neither gifts to charities nor the chance of winning lottery prizes have any impact on the response rates of mail surveys. In contrast, Fahimi et al. (2006) found that post-interview cash incentives have a positive impact on the response rate if they are of appropriate amounts, while Porter & Whitcomb (2003) confirmed that offering a prize – regardless of the size – to survey recipients for responding to the survey, with every recipient who responds being entered in a draw for one or more prizes, has no significant impact on the response rate of the survey. Hence, although lottery incentives in particular appear to be a popular and growing method for increasing response rates, the extensive survey research literature on post-paid and lottery incentives indicate that they have little or no impact on survey response rates, or that if they have an effect this is found to diminish as the size of the prize is increased (Warriner et al., 1996; Singer et al., 2000; Ryu et al., 2006). This finding has led Göritz (2004) to conclude that lottery prizes are less cost-effective than originally anticipated.

Because the majority of households in developed countries – 93 percent in Denmark – have an internet connection, which they know how to use in an efficient way, world wide web surveys have become more commonly used as a data collection instrument. This development is also due to the fact that web interviews are less costly than mail or telephone interviews, and that the results are available for analyses immediately after the questionnaire has been completed and submitted. Although web surveys offer the respondent the opportunity to participate at a time of the day most appropriate for her/him, avoiding problems such as being called for a telephone interview while eating a meal or watching a favourite TV programme, the drawback of web interviews is the relatively small response rate compared to other data collection modes (Couper, 2000). This has made the importance of incentives to encourage participation in web surveys even greater, and a large number of experiments have been performed to investigate whether they work. In a meta-analysis Göritz (2006) found that material incentives promote responses and participant retention in web surveys, and that the retention rate, i.e. the share of the sample contacted who continue participating until the end of a survey, is higher when incentives are employed. Whether or not these incentives are cost-effective depends on the returns desired in terms of minimizing the cost per participant or reducing non-response error, and also, obviously, on how expensive the incentives and the survey are in general.

To increase the response rate, most surveys include a reminder call procedure, sometimes organized as a separate follow-up phase with its own incentives. Fahimi et al. (2006) showed in an experiment that not only do incentives increase the response rate during the first phase of data collection, but also that the completion rate during a CATI follow-up phase of data collection is increased. Moreover, an early response incentive during the first phase that encouraged web interviews resulted in a high proportion of the interviews being done via the web. Fahimi et al. also found that, on average, the cost per completed interview is lower when incentives are offered, and that this reduction easily offsets the added cost of the incentives.

Some important factors related to survey quality are the number of questions replied to (Göritz, 2005), the speed at which responses are submitted (Galesic et al., 2008) and the provision of replies to sensitive questions (Kreuter et al., 2008). It is believed that both the mode of interview used and the incentives used to improve response rates, i.e. response quantity, have an impact on the response quality. With incentives paid post-interview it is possible to make receipt of the incentive contingent on the completeness of the questionnaire submitted. Göritz (2005) carried out an experiment in which some people were invited to participate in a survey where all participants were eligible for the incentive – an unconditional incentive – and some other people were invited to participate in a survey where only those who answered every question asked received the incentive – a contingent incentive. The outcomes were reported in terms of response rates, retention rates, number of omitted closed-ended items, length of answers to open-ended questions, and stereotypical answering of grid-like question batteries. The result was that contingent incentives decreased responses to the study compared to unconditional incentives, and that the quality and retention were no different in either case.

Another study by Göritz (2004) on the impact of incentives for online access panels showed that redeemable bonus points, money lotteries or gift lotteries had an impact on response quality and survey outcome, although the attrition rate was lower when bonus points were offered in comparison with the lottery incentives. Moreover, whether the prize in a cash lottery is given as a single payout or split up into several prizes has been found to have no impact on response and retention rates in online panels, nor does the amount of the prizes affect these rates (Göritz, 2006). Finally, it has been found that the promise of payment for participation in each wave in an online panel has a negative effect on responses in wave one, but a positive effect on responses in wave two (Göritz et al., 2008), a possible interpretation being that people do not want to commit themselves too much, but once participating they feel committed to continue, and even more so if given the right incentive.

It might also be that web survey respondents are more likely to enter answers without giving them much thought, thereby producing data of lower quality. Heerwegh & Loosveldt (2008) show that compared to face-to-face interviewees, web survey respondents produce a higher "don't know" response rate, differentiate less on rating scales, and produce more item non-responses. Whether this also holds if the web is compared with telephone interviews is an open question, however.

Finally, the discussion of the impact of incentives and mode of data collection is only important if the non-response biases in estimates are directly related to non-response rates, and/or one mode of data collection is more cost-effective than the other. To be more precise, there only exist a problem if the survey variable under consideration is correlated with the propensity to respond. Groves (2006) argues that this is not necessarily the case, although one always has to be aware of the problem within probability sample surveys. For the survey discussed in this paper, we were able to correct for these biases through a weighting procedure developed by Statistics Denmark and based on information from administrative registers. However, this does not completely remove sampling biases within the Danish Time Use and Consumption Survey, for which reason efforts were made to improve the quality of this survey, including the use of financial incentives and different modes of data collection.

3. Data and method

Data

In order to carry out the study of daily time use and consumption in Danish families (with special emphasis on children), a sample of 6,000 adults (ages 18-74) was drawn from administrative registers held at Statistics Denmark. Some of these people had also participated in the Danish Time Use Survey of 2001, of whom some again had participated in the Danish Time Use Survey of 1987. New respondents were included to compensate for attrition and to keep the same age range, and also to provide a greater number of interviews in 2008/09 than in the previous time-use surveys.

The respondents received a letter offering them the choice of a telephone interview lasting 10-15 minutes or completion of a questionnaire on the web (an access code was provided for this)[1]. Respondents were also asked to complete two forms for daily time use – one for a weekday and one for a weekend day – together with an accounts booklet. If respondents in the 18-74 age group had a spouse or cohabiting partner and/or children aged 12-17, these people were also asked to complete the forms for time use. In the case of children aged 7-11, parents were asked to assist in completing a form which included time use information. Finally, a booklet for information about the previous month's spendings on goods and services and about regular costs and durable goods bought within the previous year was to be filled out for all household members.

Thus, the survey included three different instruments: Q_{hm}; D_{hijm}; E_{hm}, where Q is the questionnaire, D the diary[2], E the Booklet[3] – expenditures for the household – and h represents the household, i the individuals/household members older than 6 years, j the diary day – weekday or weekend day - and m the method used – telephone or web.

The choice between using the web (access codes were as mentioned above provided

---

[1] If Statistics Denmark had not received the web interview after a week, the respondent was called and asked to complete the form. Respondents were also offered the option of an immediate telephone interview.
[2] Information on primary activities the respondent was engaged in for every 10-minute period during a designated weekday and weekend day (2*144) together with information on who the respondent was together with, if anyone, during these periods (2*144).
[3] Accounts for all expenditures on everyday goods bought by the household members within the previous month, as well as for expenditures on regular spending and durable goods bought within the previous year. Goods and services bought for the IP, spouse, children or people outside the household were assigned to the relevant person.

in the introductory letter) or being called for a telephone interview conducted by an interviewer from Statistics Denmark Survey was voluntary, and it was possible to move between the two modes in the course of the survey.

A pre-coding system was used for both time use (the day was divided into 10-minute intervals) and types of consumption, and this enabled the respondents and/or the interviewer to make electronic searches on key words, etc. This was intended to ensure more consistent processing of the responses, while also greatly reducing the subsequent work of coding in comparison with previous surveys.

The interviews were conducted at regular intervals over twelve months, covering the period March 2008 to March 2009. By linking the information obtained with register information from Statistics Denmark, it will be possible to study time use, consumption, income, family situation, attachment to the labour market, use of primary and secondary health system, etc. for around 10,000 people living in Denmark (inclusive of immigrants living in Denmark for more than seven years or with Danish citizenship).

Method

As the interview included different phases with different instruments for different family members, strenuous efforts were made to achieve the greatest possible number of completed interviews (i.e. the highest possible response rate[4]) by introducing refusal conversion incentives, see Table 1.

Table 1 Incentive experiments with DTUC

Week number/Month and year	Experimental condition	Experimental condition
	Letter	Incentives
Weeks 16-39 April to September 2008	Announcement of incentives in the final letter only	Monthly prizes: 1 DKK 5,000, 2 DKK 1,000 Expected average payout per person: DKK 17.5
Weeks 40-15 October 2008 to March 2009	Announcement of incentives in all three letters	Monthly prizes: 1 DKK 10,000, 1 DKK 5,000, 1 DKK 2,000 Double amounts for web use Expected average payout per person: DKK 42.5; web use DKK 85.0
		Follow-up: cinema tickets for all participants in the family

---

[4] Response rate = completed interviews / (completed interviews + respondent refusals + non-interviews (phone never answered, language barriers, incomplete interview, permanent health problems, etc.)).

In the first six month of the survey (April 2008 to September 2008), the respondents interviewed participated in a lottery with three prizes, one of DKK 5,000 and two of DKK 1,000 net of tax, provided they filled out all the instruments – questionnaire, diaries and booklet – either via the web or by participating in telephone interviews, with different combinations of response methods allowed. Notice of the lottery prizes was first given in the announcement letter for the booklet, the sending out of which was dependent on earlier participation in both questionnaire and diary. To further increase the response rate, the lottery prizes were increased from October 2008 so that participants could now win DKK 10,000, 5,000 or 2,000 for the completion of all the instruments, and if they used the web throughout the prizes were doubled to DKK 20,000, 10,000, or 4,000 net of tax. This is a sizeable amount of money, as the average monthly disposable income for a family in Denmark was DKK 15,400 in 2007.[5] At the same time, notice of the lottery was given in all three announcement letters. The arguments for doubling the prizes for participants using the web instead of participating in a telephone interview were that the web is more cost-effective from a research perspective, and that preliminary analyses suggested that the quality of the interviews obtained was higher using this method.

To increase the number of spouses and children participating in the time-use part of the survey, they were included in the lottery weightings, thus increasing the chances of winning the prizes for households with participating spouses and children.

Finally, the ordinary follow-up call procedure, with up to nine reminder calls per instrument per participant, was supplemented from week 40 in 2008 with the offer of cinema-tickets to all the survey participants in the family if they filled out the remaining non-completed instruments, i.e. diaries and/or the booklet.

---

[5] Own calculations based on data from Statistics Denmark.

4. Results

A. Descriptive statistics

A.1 Response rates

Table 2 shows the overall response and cooperation rates for the different instruments used in the DTUC survey. We see that the response rate was fairly high compared to other questionnaire-based surveys, with 77% of the respondents completing the questionnaire either on the telephone or via the web, and 80% of the respondents contacted actually cooperating/participating in the survey. The corresponding response rate for the questionnaire in the Danish Time Use Survey 2001 (Bonke, 2002) was 65-67%.

Table 2 Number of interviews and unconditional and conditional response rates

	Q	D (IP)	E
Number of interviews (completed)	6,091	3,755	3,575
	Response rates[1] (cooperation rates[2])		
- unconditional	77 (80)	48 (51)	45 (47)
- conditional on Q		62	59
- conditional on D			84

[1]Includes non-contacts in the denominator
[2]Excludes non-contacts in the denominator

The response rate for diaries filled out by the IP him/herself is more modest, namely 48, which is close to that obtained in the DTUS-2001 (.49). For the booklet the response rate was 45, which is similar to that of the ordinary Danish Household Expenditure Survey. This gives response rates conditional on having filled out the questionnaire of 59 for the booklet and 62 for the IP's diaries. There was a good level of retention; 84 of the IP diary respondents or their spouses also filled out the booklet.

For couples the number of diaries to be completed was doubled, and if they had children over six years of age the number of diaries was even higher. Obviously, the response rates for spouses and children were expected to be lower than that for the IPs, and this is indeed what we found (Table 3). While the IP response rate was around .65, the spouses' response rate was .56 and that of children .45. However, the presence of children did not impact on the parents' response rates – couples without children and couples with children had approximately the same response rates. Nor did the diary day – weekday or weekend day – have any impact on the IPs' and spouses' response rates, whether they were parents or not.

Table 3 Diary response rates for couples with and without children

	Diary day 1	Diary day 2
Couples without children		
IP	.65	.65
Spouse	.56	.55
Couples with children		
IP	.66	.65
Spouse	.57	.57
Child(ren)	.46	.45

[1] % of couples with at least one child >6 years old

A.2 Response modes/methods

The number of respondents using the web was considerable higher for the questionnaire than for the diaries and the booklet, which is surprising because the two last instruments are more time-consuming and thus more appropriate to be filled out at a time of the day most convenient to the respondent, i.e. with the lowest opportunity cost in terms of time. Nonetheless, the proportion of web completions was more than 50 percent higher for the questionnaire, with one third of participants using the web (.33) compared to only around one fifth (.20 and .23) for the diaries and the booklet.

Table 4 Interview methods for Q, D and E

	Q		D (>0)		E	
	# inter-views (IP)	Per cent	# inter-views (IP / All resp.)	Per cent	# inter-views (IP)	Per cent
Telephone (m=1)	4,059	.67	3,005/ 5,776	.80 / .79	2,757	.77
Internet (m=2)	2,032	.33	750/ 1,570	.20 / .21	818	.23
	6,091	100.0	3,755/ 7,346	100.0	3,575	100.0

The respondents were given the opportunity to choose the methods most convenient for them to use for the different instruments; 33% used a combination of methods (Table 5). The majority of these respondents (just over 50%) switched from web to telephone, which is surprising because keeping to the web mode would have given them the chance to win a double prize, at least for the period after week 40 – but in fact fewer respondents stuck to one instrument after this period, though the share of respondents who used the web for all three rounds was twice as high as before week 40. Also a considerable share of respondents went from telephone to web (25%), and, finally, the same share of respondents switched back and forth between the modes (25%). The majority of respondents kept to the same mode

Table 5 Method combinations, IP

Q	D (>0)	E	# interviews	Percent
Telephone	Telephone	Telephone	1,795	57
Web	Web	Web	300	10
Telephone	Web	Web	107	3
Telephone	Telephone	Web	158	5
Web	Telephone	Telephone	412	13
Web	Web	Telephone	118	4
Web	Telephone	Web	159	5
Telephone	Web	Telephone	100	3
			3,149[1]	100.0

1. The reason for this number being smaller than that of the total number of booklets is that some respondents filled out the booklet but not the diary.

Table 6 Who were the web users? (IP) Probit regressions

	Questionnaire		Diary		Booklet	
	Coeff.	SE	Coeff.	SE	Coeff.	SE
Female (male)	-.044	.035	.046	.050	.002	.049
Incentive	.299***	.034	.482***	.049	.277***	.048
Couple (single)	.255***	.044	.308***	.063	.359***	.063
Children (no children)	-.171***	.043	-.272***	.061	-.298***	.060
Age (<25 years old)						
25-44 years old	-.015	.090	.090	.144	.200	.135
45-59 years old	.047	.091	.168	.144	.304*	.136
≥60 years old	-.174~	.103	.019	.159	.061	.148
Education (no education)						
- vocational	.263***	.052	.116	.077	.201**	.073
- short further	.746***	.055	.487***	.078	.450***	.076
- long further	.705***	.066	.445***	.095	.283**	.094
Labour market status (OLF)						
Working	-.015	.061	.170*	.084	.064	.083
Unemployed	-.258*	.118	.129	.174	-.075	.174
Student	.441***	.105	.329*	.154	.339*	.148
Computer	.0621	.065	.211*	.098	.295**	.100
Constant	-1.119		-1.925		-1.799	
Log likelihood	-3648.37		-1747.57		-1834.25	
N:	6089		3754		3574	
Pseudo R^2	.059		.065		.045	

Significant ~.1 level *.05 level ** .01 level ***.001 level

throughout the survey; however, there were five times as many instances of respondents doing all the interviews by telephone than respondents doing all the interviews via the web (51.7% vs. 10.0%).

The proportion of Danish households with access to the Internet in 2009 is 93%, which means that most Danes are able to use this interview mode from their home. For the 7% of the population without this access, workplace computers and computers at libraries were in some cases available to respondents for replying to the survey. Nonetheless, we found that having a personal computer significantly increased the likelihood of using the web for filling out the diaries and the booklet (Table 6). Education was also a significant factor for use of the web, including filling out of the questionnaire. For couples relative to singles, the web was more popular for all the instruments – questionnaire, diary and booklet. Having children, however, decreased the likelihood of using the web for all the three instruments, although the web might well have been the most appropriate method for giving the response at a time of the day when the children were not present.

B. Response quantity – incentives and methods

The response rates over the survey period are shown in Figure 1. We see that there was some seasonal variation, with a lower response rate during the summer period and a higher response rate over the rest of the year. Moreover, a steep increase was seen at the beginning of the survey period, probably due to the fact that the interviewers became more familiar with the questions after a short time. Another interesting finding is that at the time of the changes in incentives the response rates went up for all the three instruments used in the survey, which is what we expected to be the outcome of introducing these incentives. Hence, the doubling up of the lottery prizes from week number 40 onward seems to have had a tremendous impact on the response rate for the diaries, as can be seen from the level of the solid line in relation to that of the dotted line in Figure 1.

To investigate the impact of the introduction of incentives in the survey – the experiment – in more detail, we apply a regression discontinuity (RD) design, as used in the programme evaluation literature (e.g. Heckman et al. (1999) and Lee & Card (2006)). The basic idea behind the RD design is the notion of the appearance of a threshold on a continuous scale – in our study, this scale is the week number in which the participants received the invitation to participate in the study, and the threshold occurred at week 40, when the incentive was introduced. We argue that since respondents on either side of the threshold (weeks 39 and 40) can be assumed to be almost identical in general characteristics – they are chosen randomly from Danish central population registers – the effect of the incentives can be estimated by estimating the difference in the response rates for the periods on either side of the threshold.

Figure 1 Response rates for the different instruments used in the survey during the period 1 April 2008 – 1 April 2009.

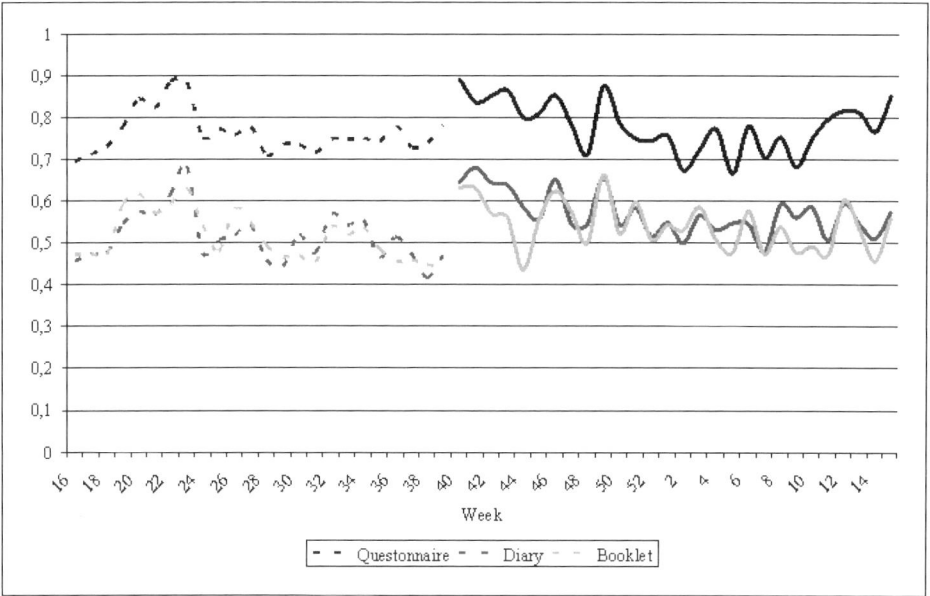

Using the notation from Heckman et al. (1999), we let Y_1 represent the response rate for individuals who have received the offer of the incentive ($t \geq 0$), and Y_0 the outcome if incentives have not been offered ($t < 0$). Since Y_1 and Y_0 cannot be simultaneously observed at any t, we instead observe $Y = D_t Y_1 + (1-D_t)Y_0$. We wish to estimate an effect of the incentive, $E[Y_1 | D_t = 1] - E[Y_0 | D_t = 1]$, by estimating both the effect on an individual who received the incentive, $E[Y_1 | D_t = 1]$, and the counterfactual observation for an individual who participated while the incentive was offered, but did not receive the incentive, $E[Y_0 | D_t = 1]$. Since the counterfactual cannot be observed, we instead use $E[Y_0 | D_t = 0]$ and extrapolate by assuming that the trend for the pre-incentive subsample would have continued into period $t = 0$ if the incentive had never been offered.

Since the incentive was introduced in week 40 and the survey ran for 52 consecutive weeks (week 16, 2008 – week 15, 2009), we cannot completely correct for seasonal variations in the behaviour of the respondents. For that reason we only look at data collected from 10 weeks before to ten weeks after the introduction of the incentive, i.e. from week 30 to week 49. Because some of the respondents contacted in weeks 44-47 were repeaters from a time use survey in 2001, we included a dummy to account for the non-random sampling of this group. A number of covariates to describe gender, ethnicity, family composition, etc. were also used as controls. Since we assume that the time trend does not change with the introduction of the incentive, we have the following model:

$$Y_{ij} = \beta_0 + D_t + \beta_1 t + D_{44-47} + \beta X_i + e_i \tag{1}$$

where Y_{ij} is the response rate for individual i in the month j, β_0 is the general intercept, D_t is a dummy for the incentive, $\beta_1 t$ is the time trend for t, D_{44-47} is the dummy for repeaters in week 44-47, βX_i is a group of covariates, and e_i is the individual error term.

Since the characteristics of the respondents who choose to participate in the questionnaire may vary according to whether they have been offered the incentive or not – people who participate due to altruistic considerations are different on observables from people whose participation is motivated by selfish factors – we cannot simply evaluate the effect of the incentives based on the parameter estimate of D_t. Instead, as mentioned earlier, we estimate the difference in average response rates between individuals who received the incentive and the counterfactual observation, thereby taking the possible change in respondents' make-up into account. Hence, what we term the *average treatment effect of the treated* (ATE) is calculated as follows for the effect of the incentive in the period t = 0:

$$\text{ATE} = E[Y_1 \mid D_t = 1] - E[Y_0 \mid D_t = 1] \tag{2}$$

Table 7 RD estimation for ATE on incentives. Probit model

	Probit	
	Coeff.	SE
Incentive	.329**	.107
Migrant	-.506***	.108
Female	.121*	.052
Has children	-.011	.068
Couple	.275***	.061
Age (<25 years old)		
25-44 years old	.031	.104
45-59 years old	-.019	.101
≥60 years old	.001	.106
Weeks 44-47	-.098	.084
Time	-.002	.009
Constant	.437	
N:	3,003	
R^2	.028	
ATE:	.103	

*p < .05; **p < .01; ***p < .001

In Table 7 we use an Probit model to estimate the impact of the incentive and the treatment effect. We find the effect to be just over 10 per cent. We have also made the estimations using data from the entire period of the survey,[6] as well as for the same period but not including the dummy for the respondents who also participated in 2001. Both estimations produced similar results. The results were also reproduced using an OLS estimator, which gave the same results.

Figure 2 Ratio of instruments completed via the web relative to those completed by telephone during the survey period 1 April 2008 – 31 March 2009.

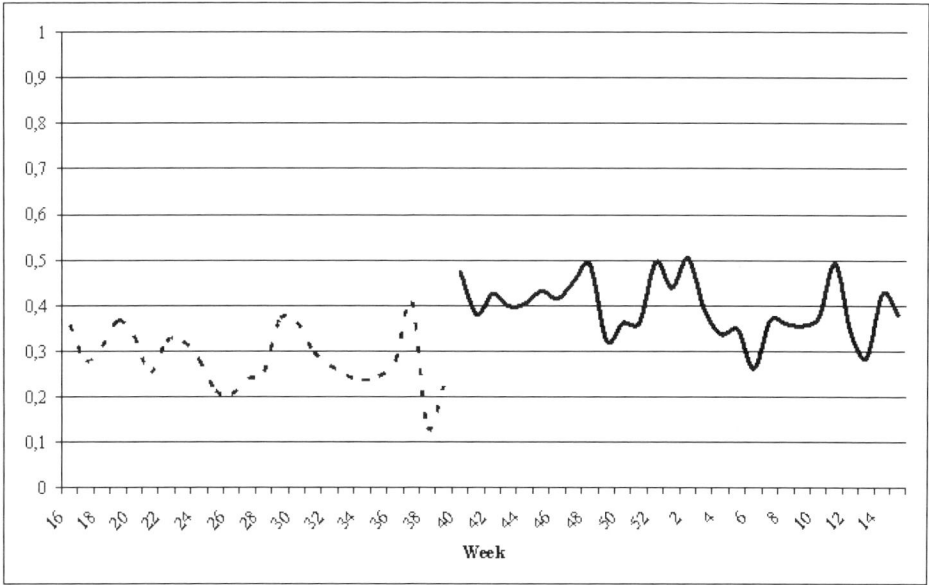

We have also calculated the ratios of questionnaires completed via the web relative to those completed by telephone throughout the period of the survey, as shown in Figure 2. Although the proportion of web-completed questionnaires was considerably higher after the doubling of the lottery prizes for respondents who completed all the instruments via the web – i.e. after week 39 – we cannot separate the direct impact of this incentive from the indirect effect of the higher response rate for the whole survey.

C. Response quality – incentives and methods

Several studies have shown that using the web mode leads to lower response quality than telephone and mail modes (Couper, 2000; Dillman & Bowker, 2001). Hence, the question to be considered is whether the lower quality of the responses

---

[6] Here we also controlled for respondents interviewed in weeks 20-23 who were also participants in the 2001 survey. We also controlled for the Christmas period, where both interviewers and respondents were assumed to be less active.

outweighs the lower cost of doing a web survey; in other words: are web interviews cost-effective? Obviously, this depends on the expected return to the investment, which is not usually explicitly stated beforehand.

In the following, we first examine whether the web questionnaire, diary and booklet information obtained in the present survey – DTUC – are of the same quality as the information obtained by the telephone interviews. Next, we investigate whether the experiments carried out in the survey had any impact on the quality of the outcome of using the different instruments, the point being that on the one hand, it is believed that the more people think they could win, the more careful they are in responding to the survey questions, while on the other hand, the larger the number of people who respond, the more likely it is that some respondents who are careless or indifferent in answering questions will participate, thus damaging the quality of the information obtained. Because of selection issues we are not able to obtain an estimate of the effect of the experiment on data quality, since we, as mentioned earlier, have no way of distinguishing between those who would have participated in the survey without the offer of incentives and those who would not have done so.

The number of non-response items is often used to measure response quality of a questionnaire, working on the assumption that the more questions there are with no responses, the lower is the quality of the survey (see for example Singer et al., 2000). We do the same here by looking specifically at three questions that we believe might have been problematic, either because it is difficult to recall the information required or because they demand sensitive information. These questions concern 1) the number of holiday weeks taken the previous year, 2) expenditures on personal consumption in the previous year, and 3) personal income net of tax in the previous year.

Table 8 Questionnaire - Number of completed questions by method

Distribution of variable	Number of completed questions (1-3)				
	Answered 0	Answered 1	Answered 2	Answered 3	Total
Number of respondents	3	64	743	5,281	6,091
	Mean number of questions answered				
Telephone	2.79				
Web	2.96				
Ho: Diff = 0	t-value: 16.30, Pr < 0.001, df: 6,098				

Table 9 Diary – Number of activities and sequences by method

	Number of sequences (1-144)	Number of activities (1-37)
Telephone	14.97	9.10
Web	16.09	10.95
Ho: Diff = 0	t-value: -11.18 Pr: <.0001 df: 12,336	t-value: -33.44 Pr: <.0001 df: 12,336

Table 10 Expenditures E – Number of goods and assigned goods by method

	Number of goods	Number of assigned goods
Telephone	14.89	13.77
Web	17.28	16.48
Ho: Diff = 0	t-value: -111.92 Pr: < 0.001 df: 3573	t-value: -13.93 Pr: < 0.001 df: 3573

The results are shown in Table 8, where we see that the great majority of respondents gave answers to all three questions, and that the mean number of positive replies was significantly higher among web users than among respondents interviewed by telephone. This result remains significant when we control for socio-economic characteristics such as sex, marital status, age, education and labour market attachment (Table 11). We therefore conclude that the use of the web yields a higher response quality than telephone interviews. At the same time we find that for the questionnaire, the introduction of incentives actually decreases quality for the respondents using telephone interviews – but because of the inherent selection problem introduced with the incentives, we cannot imply a causal relationship between the incentive and the quality of the telephone-based responses. However, it should be noted that the rise in numbers of responses on the web was greater than the rise in the response rate, which implies that either the respondents who yielded a high quality in their responses were more prone to use the web – thereby creating a selection effect – or that the respondents who would not have participated had the incentives not been offered generally gave a poorer quality of answers to difficult or sensitive questions.

The response quality of the diaries is measured as the number of different activities recorded during the day and the number of activity sequences performed (the same activity may be performed several times a day), assuming that these numbers are, among other things, a function of the respondent's accuracy in filling out the diary. Hence, it is assumed that the more the respondent is able to choose the time of the day for making the response, the more accurate he or she will be, investing more effort in recalling what happened during the day(s) concerned. Finally, we look at the ratio between different activities and sequences, to remove the possibility of autocorrelation between the two measures – i.e. the more sequences reported, the more different events are also reported.

Table 11 Questionnaire Q – Number of completed sensitive questions. Probit.

	Number of completed questions (3 or <3 questions completed)	
	Coeff.	Robust SE
Method (web=1)	.622***	.083
Incentive	-.334***	.047
Method*Incentive	.597***	.120
Female	-.241***	.045
Couple	-.054	.053
Children	.045	.059
Age (<25 years old)		
25-44 years old	.722***	.103
45-59 years old	.579***	.100
≥60 years old	.427***	.114
Education (no education)		
- skilled	.106~	.058
- short further	.217**	.066
- long further	.102	.085
Labour market status (OLF)		
Student	.082	.124
Working	.066	.076
Unemployed	.008	.129
Constant	-.561	
Log Likelihood	-2109.92	
N:	6091	
Pseudo R²	0.116	

Significant ~.1 level *.05 level ** .01 level ***.001 level

As we found for the questionnaire, the response quality was higher when respondents used the web relative to participating in a telephone interview. This is shown by Table 9 where the number of activities as well as the number of sequences is seen to be significantly higher when using the web mode than when using the telephone mode, which might confirm our expectations of greater accuracy when there is more time for making the response. When socio-economic characteristics are controlled for, we still find that the web mode is superior to the telephone mode, which also holds true for the ratio between the number of sequences and the number of different activities (Table 12). We also find indications that the incentive actually yields a larger number of sequences performed as well as a larger number of different activities – though the parameter estimates for the interaction between the incentive and reporting online indicate that this is only found among respondents interviewed by telephone. However, no similar result is found for the ratio between sequences and unique activities.

Table 12 Diary D – Number of sequences and activities. OLS regression models with clusters

	# sequences (1-144)		# activities (1-37)		Ratio[1]	
	Coeff.	Robust SE	Coeff.	Robust SE	Coeff.	Robust SE
Method (web=1)	1.282***	.262	1.920***	.145	.077***	.006
Incentive	.573***	.131	.315***	.070	.-001	.003
Method*Incentive	-.598	.340	-.334*	.185	.002	.008
Female	1.311***	.100	.892***	.056	.003	.002
Couple	.260	.168	.033	.089	-.013**	.004
Children	.840***	.149	.586***	.081	.006	.006
Age (<25 years old)						
25-44 years old	2.220***	.322	1.287***	.171	-.009	.009
45-59 years old	2.064***	.324	1.206***	.172	-.010	.010
≥60 years old	2.579***	.349	1.444***	.186	-.018~	.010
Education (no education)						
- *skilled*	-.042	.158	.061	.085	.004	.004
- *short further*	.443*	.179	.436***	.095	.009*	.004
- *long further*	.648**	.220	.448***	.115	.005	.005
Labour market status (OLF)						
Working	-.645**	.194	-.126	.100	.016	.001
Student	-.537	.379	-.051	.203	.013**	.005
Unemployed	-.510	.497	-.352	.266	.001	.010
Day (weekend = 1)	-.012	.009	-.004	.005	.000	.000
IP reported two days	.459	.491	.076	.265	-.023*	.010
Movie tickets	.115	.441	.022	.245	-.005	.012
Constant	11.186		6.390		.651	
N:	12,940		12,940		12,940	
R²	.068		.155		.094	

[1] Number of activities divided by number of sequences
Significant ~.1-level *.05-level ** .01-level ***.001-level

Table 13 Expenditures E – Number of goods and assigned goods. OLS regression models

	Number of goods		Number of assigned goods		Ratio	
	Coeff.	Robust SE	Coeff.	Robust SE	Coeff.	Robust SE
Method (web=1)	1.284***	.259	1.616***	.256	.026***	.003
Incentive	.080	.155	.-.072	.156	-.011*	.004
Method*Incentive	.363	.353	.505	.347	.012*	.004
Female	-.044	.143	-.178	.143	-.009*	.003
Couple	3.521***	.169	3.041***	.168	-.018***	.004
Children	.520**	.183	.325~	.183	-.012***	.003
Age (<25 years old)						
25-44 years old	2.167***	.435	2.068***	.496	-.014~	.008
45-59 years old	2.694***	.440	2.453***	.420	-.023**	.008
≥60 years old	2.001***	.476	1.719***	.458	-.033**	.010
Education (no education)						
- vocational	1.565***	.202	1.557***	.201	.007	.005
- short further	2.840***	.220	2.915***	.221	.018***	.005
- long further	3.347***	.296	3.429***	.268	.020***	.006
Labour market status (OLF)						
Student	.558	.483	.680	.467	.017~	.009
Working	1.888***	.241	1.739***	.243	-.001	.005
Unemployed	.859	.520	.579	.523	-.011	.014
Cinema Tickets	.788~	.503	.791	.520	.002	.010
Constant	7.034		6.712		.961	
N:	3579		3579		3579	
R^2	.355		.328		.064	

Significant ~.1-level *.05-level ** .01-level ***.001-level

Finally, the response quality of the booklet was higher when the web was used relative to the quality when the telephone was used, in the sense that more goods and services were reported using the former than the latter mode (Table 10). We looked at both reported goods in general and reported assigned goods (where the respondents indicated for whom the item was bought), and also the ratio between the two. Again, the quality differential remains significant when we control for socio-economic characteristics (Table 13). We only find an effect for the incentive when we look at the ratio, and here we find that the incentive lowers the reported 'assigned goods to all goods' ratio, but only for telephone respondents.

5. Conclusion

In this paper we have investigated the impact of incentives and the use of web-based CAPI on the response quantity and quality in a large scale Danish survey on time-use and consumption behaviour. The point of departure was that most surveys nowadays suffer from ever lower response rates and that the growing use of web-based interviews seems to intensify this problem. However, web-based surveys have several advantages over telephone and face-to-face interviews, not least in terms of cost. We therefore introduced different monetary incentives dedicated to combating this problem.

The experiment was to change the magnitude and structure of the monetary incentives after the survey had been in progress for some months, offering the new respondents larger lottery prizes than those participating in the first months of the survey. The survey was carried out over a period of one year, with around 6,000 completed interviews. Moreover, in the latter part of the survey the lottery prizes were doubled for respondents who filled out all the different parts of the survey – questionnaire, diary, booklet – using the web rather than being interviewed by telephone.

We found that large monetary incentives can have a significant effect on the general response rates in CATI and web-based CAPI surveys. We have also argued that not only can higher response rates be obtained through the use of incentives, but also that the choice of instruments – telephone or web – can be influenced when participants are offered differentiated incentives. This result is interesting, because empirical evidence shows that monetary incentives have only a limited impact on response rates, and to our knowledge no one has previously investigated the effect of differentiating the monetary incentives with the aim of prioritizing one instrument – the web – over another instrument – the telephone.

Another interesting finding concerns the response quality from using different interview instruments in large surveys. We consistently found that respondents' use of web-based CAPI yielded a higher response quality than the use of a CATI instrument. This holds for the questionnaire, where more questions were answered using the former instrument relative to the latter, for the diary, with more registered activities and sequences, and for the booklet, with a larger number of goods and goods assigned to individuals in the household obtained when respondents used the CAPI instrument rather than the CATI instrument.

The conclusion to be drawn from this experiment is therefore that not only can large monetary incentives increase the response rates in a survey, but also that the response quality may increase if one succeeds in getting more people to use the web instrument instead of being interviewed by telephone. Whether this would hold for other surveys is an open question; the survey used here was relatively complex, in that it included not only a questionnaire but also time-diaries and booklets with accounting information. It could be, however, that the effect would be as great or greater in simpler surveys.

Bibliography

Abraham, Katharina, Aaron Maitlandd and Suzanne M. Bianchi. 2006. Nonresponse in the American Time Use Survey – Who is missing from the data and how much does it matter? *Public Opinion Quarterly* 70: 676-703.

Armstrong, J. Scott. 1975. Monetary incentives in mail survey. *Public Opinion Quarterly* 39: 111-116.

Bonke, Jens (2002). *Ti dog velfærd* (in Danish). The Danish Center for Social Research. Copenhagen.

Couper, Mick P. 2000. Review: Web surveys: A review of issues and approaches. *Public Opinion Quarterly* 64: 464-494.

Crawford, Scot, Sean McCabe, Mick Couper and Carol Boyd. 2002. From mail to web: Improving response rate and data collection efficiencies. Paper presented at The International Conference on Improving Surveys, August 25-28, in Copenhagen, Denmark.

Curtin, Richard, Stanley Presser and Eleanor Singer. 2005. Changes in telephone survey nonresponse over the past quarter century. *Public Opinion Quarterly* 69: 87-98.

de Leeuw, Edith, and Wim de Heer. 2002. Trends in household survey nonresponse: A longitudinal and international comparison. In *Survey Nonresponse*, eds. Robert M. Groves, Don A. Dillman, John L. Eltinge, and Roderick J. A. Little, 41–54. New York: Wiley.

Dillman, Don A., and Dennis K. Bowker. 2001. The web questionnaire challenge to survey methodologists. In *Dimensions of Internet Science*, eds. Ulf-Dietrich Reips and Michael Bosnjak, 159-178. Lengerich: Pabst Science Publishers.

Fahimi, Mansour, Roy Whitmore, James Chromy, Peter Siegel, Margaret Cahalan, and Linda Zimbler. 2006. Efficacy of incentives in increasing response rates. Paper presented at the Second International Conference on Telephone Survey Methodology, January 11-15, in Miami, FL, USA.

Galesic, Mirta, Roger Tourangeau, Mick P Couper, and Frederick G Conrad. 2008. Eye-tracking data: New insights on response order effects and other cognitive shortcuts in survey responding. *Public Opinion Quarterly* 72: 892-913.

Groves, Robert M. 2006. Nonresponse rates and nonresponse bias in household surveys. *Public Opinion Quarterly* 70: 646-675.

Groves, Robert M., and Mick P. Couper. 1998. *Nonresponse in Household Interview Surveys*. New York: Wiley.

Göritz, Anja S. 2004. The impact of material incentives on response quantity, response quality, sample composition, survey outcome, and cost in online access panels. *International Journal of Market Research* 46: 327-345.

---. 2005. Contingent versus unconditional incentives in WWW-studies. *Metodološki zvezki – Advances in Methodology and Statistics* 2: 1-14.

---. 2006. Cash lotteries as incentives in online panels. *Social Science Computer Review* 24: 445-459.

Göritz, Anja S., Stefan Stieger, and Daniel G. Goldstein. 2008. Individual payments as a longer-term incentive in online panels. *Behavior Research Methods* 40: 1144-1149.

Hansen, Kasper M. 2006. The effects of incentives, interview length, and interviewer characteristics on response rates in a CATI-study. *International Journal of Public Opinion Research* 19: 112-121.

Heckmann, James, Robert J. Lalonde and Jeffrey A. Smith. 1999. The economics and econometrics of active labor market programs. In *Handbook of Labor Economics, Vol. 3A*, eds. Orley Ashenfelter and David Card, 1865-2097. Amsterdam: Elsevier Science B.V.

Heerwegh, Dirk, and Geert Loosveldt. 2008. Face-to-face versus web surveying in a high-internet-coverage population: Differences in response quality. *Public Opinion Quarterly* 72: 836-846.

Hembroff, Larry A., Debra Rusz, Ann Rafferty, Harry McGee and Nathaniel Ehrlich. 2005. The cost-effectiveness of alternative advance mailings in a telephone survey. *Public Opinion Quarterly* 69: 232-245.

Kreuter, Frauke, Stanley Presser and Roger Tourangeau. 2008. Social desirability bias in CATI, IVR, and web surveys: The effects of mode and question sensitivity. *Public Opinion Quarterly* 72: 847-865.

Lee, David S. and David Card. 2006. *Regression Discontinuity Inference with Specification Error*. Technical Working Paper. National Bureau of Economic Research.

Porter, Stephen R. and Michael E. Whitcomb. 2003. The impact of lottery incentives on student survey response rates. *Research in Higher Education* 44: 389-407.

Pääkkönen, Hannu. 1999. Are busy people under- or over-represented in national time budget surveys? *Society and Leisure* 21: 573-582.

Robinson, John P. 1999. Activity patterns of time-diary dropouts. *Society and Leisure* 21: 551-554.

Robinson, John P. and Geoffrey Godbey. 1997. *Time for Life: The Surprising Ways Americans Use Their Time*. 1st ed. University Park, PA: The Pennsylvania State University Press.

Ryu, Erica, Mick P. Couper and Robert W. Marans. 2006. Survey incentives: Cash vs. in-kind; face-to-face vs. mail; response rate vs. nonresponse error. *International Journal of Public Opinion Research* 18: 89-106.

Schneider, Sid, David Cantor, Paul Segel, Carlos Arieira and Luu Nguyen. 2002. *Response Mode and Incentive Experiment for Census 2000*. US Census Bureau. Available at http://www.census.gov/pred/www/rpts/RMIE_2000.pdf.

Singer, Eleanor, John van Hoewyk and Mary P. Maher. 2000. Experiments with incentives in telephone surveys. *Public Opinion Quarterly* 64: 171-188.

Warriner, Keith, John Goyder, Heidi Gjertsen, Paula Hohner and Kathleen McSpurren. 1996. Charities, no; lotteries, no; cash, yes: Main effects and interactions in a Canadian incentives experiment. *Public Opinion Quarterly* 60: 542-562.